SO THIS IS CANCER?
Words of Wisdom and Epic Tales from a 20-Something with Cancer

J.L. BARKER

©2017 J.L. Barker

All rights reserved. No portion of this book may be reproduced by any means whatsoever without written permission from the author, except for the inclusion of quotations in a media review.

Although every precaution has been taken in the preparation of this book, the author assumes no responsibility for errors or omissions. Nor is any liability assumed for damages resulting from the use of the information contained herein. Although every effort has been made to ensure that the information contained in this book is complete and accurate, the author is not engaged in rendering professional advice or services to the individual reader. This information is not intended to replace the advice of a medical practitioner and consumers should always consult with a health care professional prior to making changes to diet or lifestyle. The author shall be not be held responsible for any loss or damage allegedly arising from any information or suggestion in this book. The opinions expressed in this book represent the personal views of the author.

Table of Contents

Introduction

Chapter 1 – Oh Crap, I Have Cancer!

Chapter 1.5 – Preliminary Stage

Chapter 2 – Support and Supportive People

Chapter 2.5 – Handling Supportive People

Chapter 3 – Ports, PICCS and Things

Chapter 3.5 – Doomsday Prepping: Ports and PICCS

Chapter 3.8 – Doomsday Prepping: Hair Loss and Fertility

Chapter 4 – What Time is it? It's Chemo Time!

Chapter 4.5 – Be a Jedi Master of the Chemo Treatment

Chapter 5 – A Cancer Christmas and a Lymph Node New Year

Chapter 5.5 – How to Lose your Hair with Style and Class

Chapter 6 – Valentine's Day Rollercoaster Ride

Chapter 6.5 – Dating

Chapter 7 – What to Do if you are Terminal

Chapter 8 - After Cancer and Beyond

Chapter 9 – The Aftermath

Chapter 10 – The End

Dedication

I would like to thank my family and friends for sticking with me throughout this entire process. There has been laughter, tears, and a whole lot of waiting. I couldn't have written this book or battled through cancer without each and every one of you.

Mom and Dad, thank you for supporting me and loving me through each moment of this process and all of the other moments after. You have shown so much strength and courage throughout this experience and I am inspired by you both daily. Thank you for your example as parents and Christ followers. You have shown me what it truly means to serve God and others. Dillon, I know it was hard watching your big sis go through cancer but you kept things normal and I want you to know how much that meant to me. Aunt Ginger (Heidi), thank you for always taking care of me, surprising me in my chemo chair, feeding me, and taking my blood pressure and temperature every time I see you (even 3 years after chemo). Thank you Grandma for showing this book to everyone and presenting it as your "grandbook."

I wish I could list every single person who touched my life during this time but my publisher only gave me a set amount of space and it would take 10 pages. I can't thank you all enough for baking me treats, surprising me with parties and hats, hanging out with me in public with my bald head, crying with me, praying with me, the phone calls, the Facebook messages, reading, rereading, and editing these pages, and making cancer jokes even when it was totally inappropriate but hilarious! I have the BEST friends and family in the whole world!

I also want to thank you, the readers for choosing my book as you embark on your journey. You are the reason I wrote this book. I had you in mind and I hope you will share your journey with others the way I have.

I'm looking for someone to share in an adventure ... are you ready?

Introduction

If you've picked up this book, chances are that you or some you love is going through cancer. After going through Non-Hodgkin's Lymphoma at 24 years old, I found that the best advice that I was given consisted of accurate and sometimes painful information. Instead of becoming discouraged by these realities, I was encouraged, prepared and motivated to get through one of the most difficult times of my life. I hope that by sharing what I've learned with you, I can offer some of that same encouragement to help you get through the struggle of your life.

As you read through this book, know that some of the pages are not sugar-coated. Although at times these pages will be joyful and humorous, other times they will be raw and real. Like Gandalf the Grey, I will guide you through your journey, as well as equip you with the tools necessary to fight this evil. It is my hope that you will learn from my mistakes and grow from my experiences through a collection of epic tales and words of wisdom.

This book is written using stories, made-up quizzes and checklists. I began writing this book shortly after being diagnosed. My attitudes and perspectives expressed in these pages occurred while I was in the midst of that struggle.

It's time to be honest.
The struggle is real.

You might not want to read some of what I've written and that's understandable. At the same time, you might feel relieved that someone understands. There were good days and bad days and some in-between.

I'm sorry you have to go through this. I'm sure you've been getting a lot of encouraging words and sympathetic smiles now that you or someone close to you has cancer. Despite the encouraging words of others, the bottom line is, cancer sucks.

On an odd and hopefully inoffensive note, I want to be the first to congratulate you on becoming a member of one of the most interesting and commendable groups in the world. Like it or not, you're one of us now. You now represent a particular faction of humanity that will experience a battle that most will never face. Quite frankly, the rest of the planet will never fully "get" it, but that's okay. You're in a club now with people who do.

Cancer doesn't care who you are. You may not think about it, but you are classified into many different types of groups. Here are a few examples:

Boys vs. Girls
Young vs. Old
Geeks vs. Jocks
Introverts vs. Extroverts
Jedis vs. Siths

There are plenty of other categories into which you fit but I think that gets the point across.

So, what's the difference between the cancer club and all these other exciting groups? Cancer patients, their friends and family members are bound by something that doesn't care about any of these other attributes. Cancer doesn't care if you're 5 years old or 50 years old. It certainly doesn't care if you make $30,000 or $300,000 a year. It's a purely evil force of nature that wants to hurt, well, everyone.

If you don't think you'll ever find yourself holding hands and shedding tears with a person four times your age, think again. Cancer has no boundaries. It's a constant battle against a truly evil super villain and it doesn't stop attacking until it has won or it is defeated. You are in the club now, which means this book is your weapon, an assault rifle, a lightsaber, or a sword. It's time to equip yourself and join our ranks. Together we will slay this beast.

This book is sectioned off in an easy-to-use format. The chapters begin with a personal story of mine, followed by subchapters full of words of wisdom and helpful advice. At the end of each chapter, you'll also find blank pages for you to record your notes, comments and reflections. Everyone's story and cancer is different. The bottom line is that you're not alone and that there is a possibility that even a small part of this book might make a difference in your journey. Let's begin. Arm yourselves friends … into battle we ride!

"Looking back now, I can recognize that my experiences were abnormal."

CHAPTER 1

Oh Crap, I have Cancer!

This is a story all about how my life got flipped and turned upside down. I had just finished college and been hired as a special education autism teacher in an elementary school. Although I was nervous, I was excited to start my life as a grown woman. I was 23 and I was ready to be a grownup. With diploma in hand, I raced off into the sunset of my future. Little did I know; the future was not as bright as I thought it would be.

A few weeks after graduation, I embarked on an adventure to teach English in China. I had the experience of a lifetime and made long-lasting friendships. Everything was going great when I returned. I quickly, and stressfully, set up my classroom and started my first job as an official adult.

It is a different experience, going out into the professional world. Working in an elementary school was a complete 360° from ringing up customers, listening to their complaints and putting books on a shelf for hours. I went from a short 4-hour shift at a bookstore to a 40-hour work week taking care of children with disabilities.

The school I worked at was and is awesome and the students I had, although challenging, were amazing. The first few weeks were a combination of wonderful and absolutely horrifying, as I tried to figure out my role in teaching. The amount of paperwork special education teachers have to endure is a nightmare and you often feel like you're drowning in it on a consistent basis.

I was overwhelmed and sweating like an egg frying on concrete. I started to lose sleep every night because I woke up on the hour every hour and I was breathing like I had run a mile. It was only the second week of school and I was starting to think that maybe I couldn't handle the pressure of being a teacher, let alone an adult.

Looking back now, I can recognize that my experiences were abnormal. It was strange and I felt weird. Sometimes you know when something is wrong and you can't quite put your finger on it. I had one of those feelings that told me I felt "off" and something wasn't right. Instead of looking into it quickly, I blamed it on stress and ignored my ever-growing symptoms and the chaos going on inside of me.

A few weeks later, I had to lie on the floor of my friend's classroom while her students were at recess. I was having an ocular migraine which causes your vision to cloud with black spots and yellow flashing lights. I had become sluggish, forgetful, and I felt like all the strength had been sucked out of my body.

I was so wrapped up in being a first-year teacher and trying to keep peace in and out of my classroom, that I kept ignoring the crappy, "something is wrong," feeling. As the British say, I kept calm and carried on.

It wasn't until I started showing physical signs that I finally scheduled an appointment with my doctor. I had grown a hard, marble-like knot behind my right ear and I thought maybe my body was fighting an infection that I had picked up from one of my students.

My primary physician looked at the knot, gave me the phone number of an ear, nose, and throat specialist, and told me to call him if it got any bigger. Thinking I was merely sick or having an allergic reaction, I continued to ignore the little knot until October. I had my reasons for ignoring the knot and, trust me, they seemed perfectly reasonable at the time.

I told myself I would check it out over Thanksgiving break a few months away and continued ignoring the lump. My 24th birthday was in October, along with Grandparents Day, Halloween, first quarter progress reports, and parent teacher conferences. I was stressed, to say the least, and my health was the last thing on my mind.

Obviously, I was too busy to get it checked again, right? I couldn't have been more wrong. I wish I could take a time machine back to October and tell my past self to go to the specialist. Health is always more important and I learned that the hard way.

I was getting ready for a parent teacher conference and stopped by the speech and language pathologist's room to complain and look for chocolate. My friend was shuffling papers at her desk and I walked right in and made myself at home, as usual. We started talking about school, life, and Harry Potter when she noticed a giant lump growing just under my chin on the other side of my neck. I touched my neck, noticing it for the first time and trying not to panic. She quickly got out a flashlight and tongue depressor and checked my tonsils. They weren't swollen and she had a worried look that made me finally realize that it was time to investigate what was going on with me.

My friend insisted I call the phone number of the ear, nose, and throat doctor and schedule an appointment. An hour later, I was waiting with my Dad at a hospital for an emergency consultation.

As we waited in a tiny room, my Dad checked his emails and I stared at a picture on the wall that I can't remember now. I was thinking about all the things I still had to do at work. Then, the doctor walked in. I thought he was cute. When I told my friends about him, they gave him a lovely nickname and so for this book he will be known exclusively as the "Hot Doctor."

The Hot Doctor examined my neck and gave me a list of daunting possibilities. I listened to most of them and when he said the word, "cancer," I didn't give it much thought. The options were as follows:

A. Mononucleosis
B. Disease from my visit to China
C. Cancer

I smiled and told him whatever it was, I would be ready, and I was being honest. I put my game face on. Determined that I hadn't picked up anything menacing in China, I wanted to start checking things off the list.

First, the Hot Doctor prescribed two weeks of heavy-powered antibiotics that made me nauseous. Strange Chinese diseases were ruled out. I was relieved, knowing that I could safely return to China without worrying about disease, but the other two possibilities remained. Next, I took a mononucleosis test. Unfortunately, it was ruled out also and it was looking more and more like I had cancer.

I knew a lot about cancer going in, but it was very different than what I had previously experienced. My biological Father passed away on my 11th birthday from a rare form of thyroid cancer. I was a Daddy's girl and his death was really hard on me and my family. Although we had completely different cancers, I felt like my family was going through déjà vu.

Because two of the three possibilities were ruled out, the Hot Doctor ordered a needle biopsy. Biopsies are never fun, but you do start to get used to them. The Hot Doctor wasn't at the office when I arrived, so I was seen by an older doctor with kind eyes and a lot of swag. My Grandma had come with me and immediately he put the moves on and started flirting with her.

My grandma is a gorgeous older woman so I don't blame him, but it was the most awkward biopsy of my life. Not to mention, it was my first biopsy. While he stuck four needles into the lump, which I lovingly named "Mount Doom," he told her that she looked young enough to be my sister and that she couldn't be a day over 30. My Grandma laughed with a girlish grin and my brother watched with wide eyes while the doctor stuck four needles into the lump. It felt like a few uncomfortable bee stings.

While waiting for the results, I continued teaching every day. Everyone there was very supportive and I was more than grateful for them. Work became a second home and my fellow teachers became my family. I was at work when the Hot Doctor called to tell me that cancer cells had showed up in the biopsy. He told me we would need to take out a piece of Mount Doom so that we could decide what type of cancer it was and how it might spread.

A full biopsy was the only way to confirm what type of cancer it was. He said I'd have a scar, but I had watched enough of the Walking Dead to put together a good zombie story for an excuse. I said, "okay," and scheduled my appointment like you'd schedule a lunch date with an old friend. After I hung up the phone, I walked back into my classroom just as my students were coming in from music class. They saw me talking and crying with one of my favorite substitute teachers who happened to be there that day. They immediately started hugging me while I cried, even though they had no idea what was going on. Getting hugged by concerned-looking second graders who patted my arm and wiped my tears was exactly what I needed.

A week later I was completely naked, wearing no makeup, and lying on an operating table. My friends were giving me such a hard time about the Hot Doctor performing my surgery, that I was blushing all the way into the operating room. I was pretty sure I'd tell him that I thought he was attractive in my sleep, but as far as I know, I didn't say anything mortifying. I woke up to the sound of my own voice praying for my family and my Mom was sitting by my bedside. The nurses told me that it was sweet that I was praying in my sleep, but I was embarrassed. It made me wonder what I said in surgery.

My Mom and Dad told me that the Hot Doctor found multiple tumors on the inside of my neck and that he removed only half of the giant tumor that was easily visible. They also said the lymphoma looked like scaly opaque fish skin so it was easy to spot. I tried to push the thought of the kraken living under my skin out of my mind as I looked out the car window on the way home. The test they would do on the tumor they removed would tell us more, but at that point it didn't matter what type it was, cancer was cancer and I had it.

I was in the Hot Doctor's office a few days later. My family was gathered with me in a small room and when he came in, I could tell right away that he was upset. He sat down and told us the news. I had Diffuse Large B-Cell Non-Hodgkin's Lymphoma. I tried my best to smile and I found myself assuring everyone in the room that I would be fine. The Hot Doctor told me this was just another bump in the road of life and that I would beat this. I believed him and he was right.

After words of encouragement and plenty of tears, I was so thankful it was his office that I stepped into a month prior. He set me up with an oncologist at the University of Kansas who had an office directly across the street from his office. It was called the Cancer Center. Even better, the offices were 5 minutes from my house. Although things were looking grim, they also were looking up. We knew what we were up against. It was time to start the fight.

"Cancer doesn't stop your life and if you establish that boundary in the beginning, it will hold true throughout the war."

CHAPTER 1.5

Preliminary Stage

These words of wisdom involving the preliminary stage are fairly simple. I wish I would have been more proactive investigating my health. Had I known that I wasn't invincible, I would have taken preventative measures long before I wound up sick. Although it might be too late for some of us, it is important to encourage our family and friends to take their health seriously. Here are some things I learned in the first stage:

1. We are not invincible—no matter how much we say, "It won't happen to me." We need to realize that nothing in life is certain. We can never fully know for sure that something will not happen to us. It is always better to take your health seriously, get regular checkups and touch base with your doctor.

2. Listen to your gut feelings—I've already noted that I had a feeling that something was off. I felt strange, like something inside of me wasn't working properly. I tried to attribute these things to stress, but I knew better. Now, every time I get a gut feeling, I listen. Even if I'm wrong, it's worth pursuing for the one time I might be right.

Words for Sidekicks (helpful family and/or friends)
If you find yourself in the "Sidekick" position as a loved one is diagnosed with cancer, there are a few things you can do to help them during the preliminary stage.

1. Just be there—your hero is about to go through a lot of different emotions while being diagnosed. Most of the time, a hero just needs a Sidekick to be in the room with them. Another warm body goes a long way.

2. Keep your loved one on track. It is more than likely that your loved one will derail and get caught up in other thoughts and feelings while being given important medical information. Keep an ear out and help them remember what the doctor said and what steps need to be taken after their diagnoses.

Advice for the first stage of your Cancer Treatment

The truth is that you're going to be doing a lot of "hurry up and wait." You'll be told it is an urgent matter, but your appointments will be scheduled for two weeks out. You will be told to get to the hospital for a biopsy right away, which will take place almost an entire week later. The whole process of the preliminary diagnosis took about a month and it was another month before I was hooked up to chemotherapy. My advice to you is:

– Try to act normal. Only think about cancer when it comes up. Don't force yourself to talk about it unless you want to. You have a life and things to do. Cancer doesn't stop your life and if you establish that boundary in the beginning, it will hold true throughout the war.

– Start writing it down. Note dates for appointments; this is important. You can have a buddy do this for you if you'd rather not, but I suggest opening up a note on your smartphone and keeping an "important date" journal. You will need this to keep track of things, as well.

A Quick Financial Side Note

It's no secret that this whole ordeal is going to cost you some cash. When you start paying off college loans, it sucks, but it's okay because you have your little piece of paper to show for it. You grin, bear it, and pay off your loan like you pay for your phone bill every month. Fortunately, you have something to show for it; your fancy smartphone. When you have chemo bills, you don't have anything pleasant to look at framed above your bed. The simple truth is that no one wants to pay to lose their hair and be poisoned. In reality, I had to pay to stay alive. Luckily, I had amazing friends and family who helped me pay off my debt. All categories of supportive people can chip in and help you raise money to lighten the debt load. A few tips about money include:

1. Delegate – Don't do your own fundraisers! People will organize these things for you, but you will have enough on your plate to think about.

2. T-Shirts are cool – I created a design and my friend made the most awesome t-shirts from the design. She paid for the initial printing and I sold the t-shirts for 20 dollars each.

3. Jewelry – I was set up with a great website, "Bravelets." This site walks you through designing and selling jewelry to raise money for your disease treatment. It was an easy way for my friends and family to donate and get a

stylish necklace or bracelet out of the deal.

Overall, my cancer treatment cost over $100,000, but with insurance, it was greatly reduced to around $18,000. There are grants you can apply for, like scholarships, and there are a lot of places that are willing to help. Don't let money stress you out; put someone else in charge for now and focus on getting through your treatment.

"People truly are amazing. They are loving, resilient, and in the face of adversity, they come together. They fight together."

CHAPTER 2

Support and Supportive People

The next few days were a blur as I awaited my appointment at the Cancer Center. My Mom called one person from each side of our family and appointed them to be the official family liaisons. It was better this way and easier on her and me. Some of my family members were experiencing the memories of another cancer call they'd had 13 years prior for my biological Father. I hate that they had to receive that call again. I tried my best to tell my friends before the news went public, but it was difficult.

It is difficult to tell your friends that you have a life-threatening illness. I texted most of them because we had already talked about the possibility and they knew what was coming. I called some of them and told some in person. Finally, I explained it all in a Facebook post and revealed to the rest of the world that my life was about to drastically change.

Facebook Post
Dear friends and family, I have recently been diagnosed with Diffuse B-Cell Non-Hodgkin's Lymphoma. I'm so sorry for those of you who are finding out through here, it's been a tough few weeks of trying to find out what's been going on. Last Friday, I had a biopsy of a lymph node on my neck and am currently sporting a pretty awesome scar. I want you all to know that I will beat this and I will continue with things as planned. This is just a bump in the road! I will continue working as an autism teacher and I will continue just being awesome in general. I will start chemo next week and hopefully, will have more details from there. I will also be blogging along the way, (hopefully I will get that up soon) to keep you all updated. Thank you for your love and prayers. Let's kick cancer's a**!

After posting on Facebook, my phone rang most of the night with supportive phone calls and text messages. I couldn't believe the overwhelmingly positive response I received. I felt empowered and loved. It was also strange, though, going up on the popularity charts so quickly. I wasn't used to being in the spotlight, not that the cancer spotlight is where anyone would actually want to be. It's just a different experience, that's for sure. It was during that time that I finally understood why the Doctor (Doctor Who) kept saving the human race as he traveled through time and space. People truly are amazing. They are loving, resilient, and in the face of adversity, they come together. They fight together.

"Support begins whenever your doctor tells you that you may possibly have cancer."

CHAPTER 2.5

Handling Supportive People

Support begins whenever your doctor tells you that you may possibly have cancer. Once you've gone home and told your family and close friends that you may be joining the battle soon, they will go into "support mode" which will look different for everyone around you. You yourself might fit into one of the following categories, as you should. This is totally natural. There is nothing right or wrong about the categories. Supportive people are unique and they will each fit into these categories in different ways. There may even be someone close to you who doesn't fit into any of these categories at all and that's ok, too.

The following categories are offered to give you a "heads-up" on what to expect from people around you and to understand how they may support you and how they are going to cope. Had I known how differently people cope in the beginning, I would have better understood what my own supportive people were thinking and feeling.

The 5 Categories of Supportive People
1. The Gatherer – Gatherers begin their journey as soon as, if not before, the doctor even suggests possibilities. My Mom is a Gatherer. She started looking on medical websites the moment the lump appeared under my chin. Gatherers will know your diagnosis, along with about six other potential diagnoses, before you even get to the doctor's office. They will also be a vital source of information for you, having read about anticipated symptoms and courses of treatment. Gatherers will remind you of doctor's appointments, fight to get you the best care that they've read about online, and they will know where to go for whatever you need. They are also the kind of people who will face your cancer with focus, intelligence, and a "Let's do this! Get it done!" attitude. The downside of being a Gatherer is that one may also gather a bunch of incorrect information online accidentally. Doctors suggest patients should avoid looking for medical information online because everyone's experience is different. When Gatherers collect information, they

may also divulge information to you that the doctor would prefer to share with you. If you are a natural Gatherer, it may be hard to fight the urge to gather information. If you start to feel stressed, it would be best to put the laptop down.

2. The Encourager – Most people fit into the Encourager category and it is the most common. Encouragers are also the most diverse group because everyone has a different encouragement style. In my life, my friends and my Dad were the Encouragers who kept me going when things got tough. You'll find that people use words, crafts, cards, Facebook, letters, gift cards and lots of food to help you along the way. When someone says they are praying for you and that it's going to get better, listen to them. They care about you and their words will mean more to you as you go along.

3. The Ostrich – The Ostrich is a person who loves you and wants to be there for you, but is in denial about the situation. They don't want to believe it is happening and, therefore, can come off as a little insensitive. My Grandma loves me very much, but she refused to see me for a long time when I was bald. It was finally after we were snowed in at my house for a few days that she let it go. It was hard on her, but she got through it and I don't hold it against her. If you have an Ostrich in your life, ruffle their giant feathers with a forced hug and let them be. They will be the closest you will have to a normal, unchanging relationship while you're sick. Trust me, you'll appreciate the normalcy after a while.

4. The Observer – The Observer waits, watches and stays in the background. They are always ready to step in and defend you or take care of you at any cost, but you might not always remember that they are there. They stay hidden for the most part and at times you might feel like they are far away. My brother is an Observer and for a while I mistook him for an Ostrich. Unlike an Ostrich, though, Observers show themselves when they are most needed and they have a lot to bring to the table. They provide a safe place to go and are most known for being someone who will listen to you. They won't respond much, but believe me, they are absorbing everything. In the months to come, they will be the ones who will see you at your worst and sit quietly next to you when all you need is another warm body in the room.

5. The Lieutenant – The Lieutenant is the one person you can count on to give you a hard time. They love you, but they are super-angry at your cancer for spoiling your young adult life. They hate cancer for this and they will let you

know it. Whether it's by making cancer jokes or their constant reminders that you need to get over it and go out on Friday night, you'll be happy you have them. There will be times when you want to just lay on the couch and puke, but the Lieutenants simply won't allow that if they are around. They will insist you get out, hang out with friends and stay up past your newly-acquired bedtime. From personal experience, everyone needs a Lieutenant to slap them out of their cancer-funk.

Fill in the following blank: If you have someone in your own life who doesn't fit into the categories above, please fill in the lines below. This is your life, your story, and it's different for everyone.

6. _____ - _____
_____
_____

Which type of Supportive Person are You?
Here is a quiz to help you realize what kind of person you are. Circle the corresponding alphabet letter and total your score.

1. When you want to go buy a new microwave, you. . .

    A. Get on Amazon and compare customer reviews/ratings.

    B. Seek out the opinions of your friends and ask what brand they are using.

    C. Give someone $50 and tell them to go get you whatever one looks good.

    D. Go to the store and pick one out.

    E. Go to the store and get the one that packs the most power and has the most features.

2. You are going to eat at a new restaurant; how did you find out about it?

    A. Television, radio, online article, billboard or magazine.

    B. You have friends who have been there and it sounds amazing.

    C. That is where everyone else is going.

    D. You heard that you can get chicken strips there, so at least you'll like something.

    E. You saw it downtown last night while fighting crime after seeing a movie.

3. Your three-year-old niece falls and scrapes her knee, you . . .

    A. Pull out bandages and antibiotic ointment you just happen to have with you.

    B. Tell her that it's going to be okay and hold her while she cries.

    C. Distract her with an ice cream cone so she'll stop crying.

    D. Watch her to make sure she's okay, but wait for her to come to you for help.

    E. Brush off her knee, throw some of your bottled water on it and tell her to go play.

4. You have to bring a gift to a housewarming party, you chose. . .

    A. Mixing bowls and utensils.

    B. A dessert, welcome mat, or flowers.

    C. Food, chips and dip, probably.

    D. Money in a card or a gift card.

    E. Knives, a can opener, or a board game for everyone to play.

5. During the party, you're the one. . .

    A. Organizing the event.

    B. Mingling in the crowd.

    C. Showing up late and leaving early.

    D. Standing in the corner people-watching and occasionally socializing.

    E. Suggesting a game and getting very competitive.

Tally up your answers and determine if you're mostly A's, B's, C's, D's, or E's.

If you selected mostly A's, you're a Gatherer; B's, you're an Encourager, C's, you're an Ostrich, D's, you're an Observer, or E's, you're a Lieutenant.

"I watched their expressions go cold and their bodies shift anxiously in their seats."

CHAPTER 3

Ports, PICCS and Things

After being diagnosed, I was sent to a new doctor at the Cancer Center. I walked into the office and immediately decided I didn't like it. This was mainly due to the terrible music playing on the overhead speakers. My parents smiled and pretended not to notice the twisted look on my face. After waiting in the lobby for 30 minutes, we spent another 30 minutes waiting in a small room with a garden picture on the wall.

My doctor was a serious woman with a thick Indian accent. She offered me her sympathy and then quickly began rattling off a list of unsettling statistics. She told me I had a sixty percent chance of survival and that this was considered a good rate. My parents calmly flipped out when she said that. I watched their expressions go cold and their bodies shift anxiously in their seats. Having researched for hours online, my mom had found that the survival rate was close to ninety-five percent. My parents gave me sheepish smiles and turned to my doctor again as she continued on with her speech.

After scheduling my next appointment to get my first round of scans, we headed back home. My parents were nervously whispering in the car about the Cancer Center and I was trying to forget about the music selection. The scans would tell us what cancer stage I was in and then we could start planning my treatment.

A week later I was sitting in a dark room drinking an unpleasant cocktail. The cocktail contained a radioactive fluid, which was meant to light up the tumors inside of me during the scan, thus making everything easier to see.

Once you are inside the machine, things go rather quickly. They give you a dye through an IV or through a port that makes you feel warm from head to toe. The technician warned me that it also makes you feel like you've wet your pants. Thankfully, you don't actually pee yourself, but they weren't joking.

Three days later, my Mom and I returned to the Cancer Center to get my results. Apparently, once in the scanning machine, I lit up like the fourth of July. (I was hoping to at least acquire some form of super-power from all the chemicals that I had already ingested over seven months, but unfortunately none of these special abilities had been developed ... yet.)

The doctor shared with us that I was in Stage Three. They had found cancer in my upper body and my stomach. She explained that I had a fast-growing cancer and that we had little time to spare. Immediately, a nurse came in with a tray full of funny-looking triangle objects with tubes jutting out of their sides. The objects were about the size of a quarter and looked like a small version of the Arc Reactor that Ironman used to keep shrapnel from reaching his heart.

The nurse explained that the tiny pieces of machinery were called "port-a-caths" and they are implanted under the skin on your chest. The port-a-cath inserted in me was called a "Power Port." The port had a tube that was connected to a major vein at the base of my neck so that the chemo could safely go through my bloodstream. In the past, ports were put in only after smaller, more commonly used, veins in the body were shot, meaning they could not handle chemo anymore. This only happened to the most severe patients and signaled that the cancer was terminal. My biological Father had one put in toward the end of his fight.

With the memory of this, the room completely clouded up as my eyes filled with tears. My Mom came over and held me as we cried together. The nurse stood awkwardly in the corner, not sure what to say as my Mom wiped my face. She kept repeating, "This isn't like Dad."

The nurse assured me the port was simply standard procedure because they have found that it was safer in the long run to implant all cancer patients with a Power Port or PICC Line. She told me that it didn't mean that I was terminal, so I choked back the rest of my tears and nodded my head.

She continued to list off the procedures I would need to go through before I would be able to start chemotherapy. She told me I would need a bone marrow biopsy, port implantation surgery, and that I would need to talk to my gynecologist to be placed on birth control pills and to discuss fertility options. I had heard that bone marrow biopsies were extremely unpleasant and I started to sweat just thinking about the surgery to come.

I was admitted for surgery a few days later to have the bone marrow biopsy and the port placement procedures. The plan was for the anesthesiologist to numb my lower back and use a new drill technique to bore into the center of my pelvis to harvest the bone marrow. Afterward, they would flip me over and insert the port into the right side of my upper chest. It was explained that I would be awake throughout the procedures, but that I wouldn't experience any pain with the help of medication.

The doctor traced his hands in the air, demonstrating the process, while I was being hooked up to the IV. He informed me that this newer drill method could not be stopped once it had broken through the skin. If the drill was stopped, the skin would catch and tear around the drill. However, the doctor assured me this was safe, far less painful and a quicker method than the original.

Unfortunately, something went terribly wrong. I was unresponsive to the medication they used and we did not find out I was unresponsive until the drilling process began. The drill entered my skin and I started screaming and grabbing the edge of the mat I was laying on. The doctor began yelling at the nurse near me and she pressed more medication into my IV and still nothing happened. I remember hearing the doctor say, "Are the meds just not working? Are you giving her enough? She hasn't passed out? I can't stop now; I'll tear her skin."

Finally, the pain ceased and I laid on the table on my stomach, so angry that I could barely speak. The nurses and doctor quickly huddled around me, apologizing and trying to make right what they had done wrong. One nurse joked that childbirth would be a breeze. Another commented on my "super-human pain tolerance." I wasn't in a joking mood though, and I could hear my Mom yelling outside the door, demanding to see me.

In moments like this, you have to decide what kind of person you want to be. I decided to be a forgiving person, even though I wanted to scream. Instead, I gave a weak smile to the staff and let them help roll me onto my now throbbing back. I asked for a different type of pain medication and then laid there shirtless and silent as they prepared my chest for the port placement.

The doctor returned from facing my parents and I could tell that he was mortified about what had just happened. He carefully approached the metal slab I was laying on and asked me the strangest question I could imagine, "Where does your wedding dress lay?"

At this point, I was starting to feel the new medication, but I wasn't so far gone that I had forgotten how incredibly single I was. I hadn't dated in over a year and there was no sign of Prince Charming in sight. I'm sure the look on my face was priceless as I gazed up at him and said, "I'm not getting married." I felt the room lighten to the sounds of mild-mannered chuckling. The doctor smiled and said, "Oh good, the new meds must be working. Sweetheart, point to where your dress starts." Confused, I pointed to a low spot on my chest and said, "Well, when I do get married, I guess it would be here." He drew a line and told me he would implant my port low on my chest so that I could cover it up with my wedding dress.

Although I was highly medicated and confused, I still felt the doctor's fingers putting the tube and futuristic machine under my skin. It did not hurt, but feeling pressure on my chest was a very interesting experience. I would not say it was a bad one, but it was a creepy one and one I've dreamt about ever since. After the procedure, they told me that I should not have any issues with the Power Port and they quickly sent me on my way. I only remember sitting in the backseat of my parents' car, staring at the passenger seat headrest and then waking up the next day in my bed. I woke up in horrible pain. I also woke up to an explanation from my Mom about my upcoming wedding; she had lied to the doctor so that he would place my port low for my dress.

They hadn't issued me any pain medication for the days to come and, as is common practice, they do not give you medication after having a port implanted. My hip felt fine, but recovering from the port implant was one of the hardest parts of the process. I wished I had asked for pain medication, but I did not. I did not have time to think about pain; I had to start preparing for chemotherapy, or as it is commonly called, "chemo."

"It's essential to always be prepared when you are in the middle of the war for your life."

CHAPTER 3.5

Doomsday Prepping: Ports and PICCS

I know that this part of the story probably wasn't the most pleasant thing to read. It's, by far, one of my least favorite chapters. You're going to encounter a lot of interesting obstacles and situations throughout your journey. During the preparing process, there are some truths and lies that you need to be aware of. It's better to be armed and prepared.

Here are two lies you may encounter:

1. Ports and PICC Lines do not hurt. When you hear the letter "P," think "possible pain." Ports and PICCs are incredibly underrated in the pain department. So much so, that they do not write you a script for pain medication. Unfortunately, ports and PICCs continue to hurt after they are implanted and at times, even after they are removed.

2. Pain medication always works. Please make sure you're well-anesthetized before the doctor starts any type of procedure that requires you to be awake.

PS. If you're a girl, make sure your mom tells you if she's going to lie to the doctor and tell them you're getting married.

The best advice I can give you is to be prepared! You have to prepare to go into battle just like you have to prepare to leave the house every day. It's essential to always be prepared when you are in the middle of the war for your life.

Be prepared to speak up for yourself if you feel something is wrong; trust your gut. It is probably doing flip-flops to get your attention, so listen to your intestines. If you feel uncomfortable, a doctor may even give you the option to be put under anesthesia. It never hurts to ask.

Be thankful that you are getting a port or PICC. I know you don't want one because I didn't either, but I'm so thankful now that I had one then. The needle will hurt going into the port, but it feels like any other shot. There is numbing cream you can put use to put on the port and that really helps.

Your Power Port, Smart Port, etc. is like having Iron Man's Arc Reactor in your chest. Iron Man has an Arc Reactor placed in his chest that uses magnetic force to keep shrapnel from reaching his heart. Unlike his, yours does not glow, but be happy to be almost Tony Stark.

Take care of your scars. Find a good scar cream, like Mederma™, or you can use Vitamin E oil to help your scars heal up nicely. Keep your scars out of the sun as much as possible and find a good sunscreen to use for protection. My neck scar was on my left side, which meant it was in the direct sun every time I drove my car. I made a habit of keeping sunscreen in my purse and slathering it on when I noticed the sun beating down through the driver's side window.

"I sat in the fertility doctor's office with my Mom thinking about things I didn't plan on thinking about for a few years."

CHAPTER 3.8

Doomsday Prepping: Hair Loss and Fertility

Before you start chemo, it is a good idea to get a game plan together about your hair. I went to a million different places trying on wigs for fun and taking crazy pictures with my Mom. The first place I went to was an upscale salon. My mom and I spent over an hour trying on wigs and laughing. I think she tried on more than me that day and came close to buying a few. We tried on every cut and color, but I was not completely satisfied with any of them. We continued shopping until we stumbled upon a very small salon in an obscure shopping center and decided to give it a shot. When we walked in, we were introduced to the manager who had been working for the salon for many years. His hair was flawless and he had to be well into his seventies. He then explained that he prematurely lost his hair in his mid-thirties and that he had been using the items from the salon ever since. He went on to tell us that he had made wigs for big-time country western stars in Nashville before coming to Kansas City to set up shop. The wigs in the salon were expensive, but they were one hundred percent human hair. The wigs could even be cut and colored, and then taped or glued onto your head so you could wear them all day, all night, or for even longer periods of time. The best part was the wigs had a fake scalp that gave the appearance of an actual hairline. Creepy and cool.

I found a wig I wanted, but I could not have afforded it without the help of my friends and family, who donated the money and supported me. The total cost was $600, which sounds like a lot, but, in actuality, was not so bad. I only wore my wig on special occasions, like Easter, girls-nights, New Year's Eve or important meetings for work. It was worth every penny to be able to wear it when I needed it most. It was definitely the way to go. I also used a special serum for my eyelashes and eyebrows called Brian Joseph's™ Conditioning Gel. It was expensive, but the gel helped me hold onto about half of my eyelashes, and my eyebrows became spotty, but never disappeared. If I had not had used that product; chances are, I would have lost every eyelash and eyebrow hair that I had. In the end, after my chemo was done, those babies came back in just as they were before, no problem.

I had the wig and hair thing figured out before I had even sat down for my first round of chemo. I'm happy I did because wig hunting was not something I would have been up for when I was sick. Accepting my hair loss was a different story. My brain was telling me to cut it off before chemo even started, but I just could not bring myself to do it. I had been dealing with many other challenges and I had pushed the subject to the back of my mind. I did not want to deal with losing my long, glossy hair. Instead, I sat at chemo with a head full of long hair and promised myself I would cut it by the following week.

Fertility and You

As mentioned in Chapter 1, I had to arrange several medical appointments before I could start chemo. One of those appointments was with my gynecologist to talk about fertility. The following section contains important information and, whether or not you've dreamt of a houseful of children or you cringe at an infant's cry, this information is critical for your future. If you do not want children now and you've never changed your mind about anything before in your life, you can skip this section. However, please know that you may meet "The One" someday and feel the need to procreate; guys and gals need to prepare now for the future ahead. I'm going to go into detail about my personal experience. I'm going to talk about eggs, but without eggs there would be no babies, so men … keep reading! Whether your significant other is the one in cancer treatment or yourself, men and women are all in this together. Therefore, both genders need to learn as much as possible to prepare for the beast that lies ahead.

I sat in the fertility doctor's office with my Mom thinking about things I didn't plan on thinking about for a few years. The doctor told me that she recommended freezing my eggs. Unfortunately, it was a two-week process and unless I had some sperm to go with my eggs, the chances of them surviving the freezing process were cut in half. As I started weighing my options and calculating the ten-thousand-dollar price tag in my head, I started to panic. I had no time, no sperm, and no money. I left the specialist feeling like part of my future had been ripped from my hands.

A few days later, I went in for my mandatory second opinion with a lymphoma and leukemia specialist downtown. The oncologist had worked with many 20-something girls with lymphoma, and hearing his side of the story took a giant weight off my chest. He looked me in the eyes, told me to not worry and to let it go. He smiled as he described my future, full of children and without the pain of infertility. As it turns out, young adult women with lymphoma and leukemia have resilient eggs and there are very few reported cases of infertility after chemo. I felt absolute relief.

I did take a few precautions before diving into treatment. Before you begin, the oncologist will want to put you on a birth control pill if you aren't already taking one. The pill will provide extra protection and you will want to stay on it throughout chemotherapy. You won't have a period while you are taking chemo, so enjoy that part while it lasts! You can expect it to return full force afterwards. For me personally, it only took a month before my cycle was back to normal. After chemo, my gynecologist told me everything was functioning and working properly and that my eggs looked happy and healthy.

I haven't tried getting pregnant yet, but I will cross that bridge when I come to it. I know that if and when God wants me to have kids, nothing is going to stand in the way of that. My husband and I will take that bull by the horns and deal with it together when the time comes, but I'm not worried. Overall, it is important to gather all the facts. Talk to your doctor about your specific type of cancer and factor in all the variables. It can take up to two weeks to harvest eggs and there is also a procedure involved. It's crucial to be proactive and not waste time. If freezing your eggs is the best option, you and your doctor can make arrangements to ensure that you have plenty of little Hobbits running around your house someday.

"I was starting to feel like Luke on Dagobah.
I wasn't sure how I was going to lift
this chemo X-Wing out of the swamp."

CHAPTER 4

What Time is it? It's Chemo Time!

I was scheduled to have my first chemo three days after my port implant and I'll admit to being pretty nervous about the whole ordeal. I woke up early that day and packed my entire room into a beach bag. I may have been a little over-prepared for my 6-hour chemo treatment. I took my laptop, my power cords, three books, a blanket, soft socks and snacks. I walked in with my Mom, who was hauling all of my cargo, and braced myself for whatever was to come.

The first thing you notice when you walk into a chemotherapy treatment center is that there is a slight level of awkwardness. The room was sectioned into four distinct pods. Each pod had six recliners sitting in a circle and facing each other. The nurses greeted me at the door and showed me to my pod. I sat in the first recliner and my Mom pulled up a chair next to me. Being the youngest person in there, I was surrounded by older (much older) patients. I felt them staring as I walked in. I know they thought they were whispering, but I could clearly hear them saying things like, "What a shame," and "She's so young." I sat there twisting my long hair and biting my lip nervously. The nurse came over and began explaining the chemotherapy treatment process. I nodded and looked at my Mom who was surrounded with my bags and smiling.

The nurse began cleaning the aching port on my chest with an orange scrub brush that leaked sanitation solution when she squeezed it. She then pieced together a long tube with a needle that was connected to a loud machine on wheels. She told me to breathe and then pressed the long needle into my port. My eyes watered because my skin had hardly healed and was tender from the surgery only days before. She taped the base of the needle to my chest so it would not come out and hooked the cord up to the IV bags in the machine. I thought the worst was over.

My chemo cocktail was called "R-CHOP," a combination of Rituxan, Cyclophos-phamide, Hydroxydaunomycin, Oncovin and Prednisone. I was told that I would be there for six to seven hours while I waited for the fluids to drain into my veins. I would be spending all day in the recliner. My treatment started off well. I began my time by reading and I got up to pee every 30 minutes because of all the liquid I was ingesting. They make you double flush the toilet because your pee becomes radioactive and they don't want other people getting your chemo cocktail on them. Although it would make a good story: "How did you get your super-powers?" "I sat in radioactive urine!"

After an hour, everything hit the fan. I got sick and I mean really sick. I started convulsing in my neck and back. I became dizzy, nauseous and I had multiple full body spasms shake through me like an earthquake. The nurses calmly freaked out while they tried to take care of me, but my body was going insane. No one was sure what was happening. I thought I might pass out, but I resisted because I did not want to scare my Mom. Later, I found out that the first round of chemo with R-CHOP is always rough. The first administration of R-CHOP technically requires the patient to be admitted to the hospital for three days. Unfortunately, when the insurance companies cut monies for this chemo treatment, the hospital stopped offering a 3-day hospital stay. Looking back, I can understand now why the preferred method to start R-CHOP is a 3-day stay. The R stands for Rituxan and it is a nasty drug. Your body gets used to it after a while, but you have to build up a tolerance.

On that first day, after three hours, the Rituxan bag dripped dry and I started feeling a little better. I was able to stomach a sandwich and I cuddled up in my Star Wars blanket. I was starting to feel like Luke on Dagobah. I wasn't sure how I was going to lift this chemo X-Wing out of the swamp. By the time my chemo session was over, I was the only patient left in the clinic. I left the clinic relieved to be done and I went home that night exhausted and determined to go to work the next day. However, around 7 pm that night, my arms became heavy and continued to tingle throughout the night. I wasn't able to sleep all night because of it and my arms did not feel better until 11 am the next day. The constant tingling was just too much to sleep through. The nurse had told me that this would happen and that it would be normal every night after chemo.

I started work the next day with tingling arms and everyone watched me closely to see if I would pass out. Three days later, sores formed on the inside of my throat and I developed a nausea that did not leave until after the cancer was long gone. After every round of chemo, I planned for my symptoms. The first night I wouldn't sleep so I watched *Lord of the Rings* all night. Days 3-6, I didn't eat hot food because of the sores in my mouth. The rest of the time, I would go to sleep early so that my body wouldn't ache in the mornings. The schedule changed at times, but mostly it was predictable and it became life.

After you have your first round of chemo, your brain can become fuzzy and you start to live in a daze. Of course, I didn't realize I was in this daze until long after chemotherapy was over and I was in remission, but reading through my journals, I can tell how incredibly high I was. You will forget things and you may space out most of the time, so for the sake of all humanity, write everything down! Sticky notes, phone notes, setting alarms, keeping a journal of side effects, and delegating a friend as your remember-all are all things you need to do as soon as you start treatment. It's best to have one person in your life become your manager. There were times when I was so fuzzy, I would tell people to contact my manager and that she would schedule appointments. My manager was my Mom. Among the many things I would forget was why I walked into certain rooms; I could not remember. Also, I could not remember whether or not I had eaten a meal. Because of this, I had too many meals because my solution was always to eat again. The days dragged on and finally, one month later, holiday break was on the horizon and so was my second round of chemo. The second round was much smoother, and I felt more prepared. I didn't have any strange symptoms and I was able to stomach the medication much better.

"I can honestly say I probably worked myself too hard. I'm happy I didn't stop though, because it gave me something else to think about besides my cancer."

CHAPTER 4.5

Be A Jedi Master of The Chemo Treatment

In this section, I've compiled a few important points to help you get through your chemotherapy sessions. You can use this list or modify it, depending on how long your treatments are. By my 6th treatment, I had become a "Master of Understanding" and knew what to expect and how to be prepared. Some of that understanding I'm now passing on to you:

Do or do not. . .
Do bring a buddy. I brought my parents, my brother, my friends, etc. Don't go through this alone.

Do bring a form of entertainment. Bring your computer, iPad, power cords, or book.

Do wear comfortable clothing. It's not a fashion show and you won't be picking up babes while you're being pumped with roids. If you're a lady, wear a little makeup when your friends are visiting because they will take pictures the entire time.

Do bring a jacket and socks. Your feet will get cold and it's always cold in buildings so, just like the movies or the mall, bring a jacket.

Do have someone bring you lunch if they offer to do so. You have cancer, dang it, you deserve Steak n' Shake, or pizza from Pizza the Hutt. Those were my go-to cravings.

Do ask for Magic Mouthwash. It's a special medicine to help with the sores you will get on your tongue and in your throat. It will save you a lot of discomfort, so get it before you leave or get a script for it.

Do bring a pillow. Unlike the clerks at gas stations during road trips, some facilities have heated blankets and pillows for your chemo journey. Until you know if you'll be getting the goods, make sure to bring a pillow with you. If you're like me, you'll use at least five heated blankets per session. Have at least three trusty blankets at home, though, to cuddle up with because you will want to do that a lot. I have a Star Wars® blanket, a lymphoma lime green zebra blanket, and an ultra-soft purple blanket with my name on it.

Do eat if you can. You will feel better putting food on your stomach to soak up and lighten the blow from all liquid poisons you are ingesting. If you puke, you will want to puke food, not acid, trust me.

. . . there is no try.
Here is a handy-dandy checklist I've compiled for your next chemo visit. Family and friends might want to consider bringing similar items if they are planning on staying the whole day. Most of the time, friends wind up talking and goofing off the whole time, but you will need some way to get on the internet so you can Facebook-stalk the people you're talking about. Eventually, during my weeks of treatment, I was moved to a private room because my friends and I were so loud. I don't think the other patients cared to hear about men and reality television.

Do I Have? Check List
____ Entertainment

____ Chargers

____ Jacket

____ Soft socks

____ Buddy

____ Delegated Lunch Bringer

Chemo & Stupid Symptoms
You're going to have a variety of chemo-related symptoms, but, for the most part, they will stay consistent after each session. I have included a page from my personal chemo journal of what symptoms I had and when they occurred. I got so familiar with them, that I knew what days I would have them, allowing me to plan accordingly. For example, I wouldn't eat spicy food on days 5-7 because that's when I had a swollen, sore covered tongue, etc. The following is what I wrote on "Chemo Diary" after my first round of chemo treatments (Days 0 – 26):

Day 0 – Severe allergic reactions during chemo. Lost feeling in arms and hands after 5 pm. Didn't sleep all night.

Day 1 – Regained feelings in arms by 11 am. Severe throat discomfort, back of throat, nausea all day. Used Magic Mouthwash to dull pain.

Day 2 – Woke up with chemo nightmares. Sore throat, jaw pain, nausea and tiredness. Slight headache.

Day 3 – Shortness of breath, chest pain, little throat discomfort and nausea. Bad headache, severe exhaustion. Slow movement, no energy. Cried for hours because I had to miss the midnight Hobbit premier for *Desolation of Smaug*.

Day 4 – First day to wake up hungry. Chest pain, shortness of breath, no throat pain until that night.

Day 5 – No energy, blurred vision, nausea.

Day 6 – Developed sore on inside of lip, swollen and painful tongue, nausea.

Day 7 – Swollen and painful tongue, nausea.

Day 8–15 – Slight nausea, tiredness, but overall feeling better.

Day 16 – Painful, tender, tingly scalp. Hair still there.

Day 17 – Hair begins to fall out in strands, head is still tender.

Day 18–25 – Overall feeling better. Leaving hair everywhere.

Day 26 – No hair, don't care.

I had monthly chemo treatments so these symptoms spread out across a few weeks. During chemo, I never stopped working, but I can honestly say I probably worked myself too hard. I'm happy I didn't stop, though, because it gave me something else to think about besides my cancer. Focusing on the kids took the focus off my health. I did have a few "medical mystery symptoms" that other people who underwent R-CHOP never experienced. The tension and spasms I experienced in the first chemo session (and thankfully the only time) was a new symptom that had never been seen before. I had another bizarre symptom during my fourth treatment where I experienced an ocular migraine for an hour or so. Everyone is different and will react differently, and, who knows, maybe you will have a symptom strange enough to be published in a medical journal like me! Good for you!

"My New Year's Resolution was: kick cancer's ass."

CHAPTER 5

A Cancer Christmas and A Lymph Node New Year

A lot can happen in just two weeks. Christmas and New Year's Eve were just around the corner, and my body was getting ready to go through a lot of changes. After my first round of chemo, I sat in my hairstylist's salon inside her home. I spun around in the swivel chair, breathing deeply and preparing myself for the next big step in my cancer process, cutting my hair for Locks of Love. I was sick from chemo and trying to hold back tears while she showed me hairstyles she had found online. I had chosen to go straight for the Emma Watson post-Harry Potter pixie cut. I sat there trying to be brave but the more that I thought about it, the sicker it made me feel. Going from long hair to a short, "boyish" hairdo was frightening, to say the least. I had never had my hair that short in my life and I was not prepared to start now. Luckily, she suggested starting with a chin length bob and holding off on the pixie until my hair started to fall out. We settled on an inverted bob.

There are moments that freeze in time and stick with you forever. Not to be dramatic, but this was one of those moments. I felt the scissors cutting a straight line across the base of my neck. I held my breath as my hair fell around my face. I sat there shocked and vulnerable. I felt like Rapunzel when Flynn Ryder cut off her hair to save her life. A second later, I began to cry. My friend put down the scissors and held me. She handed me the 13-inch ponytail and I looked at her in the mirror and said, "We did it." She smiled through tears and said, "There's a little girl out there who's going to love this." I still think about that moment. Wherever that little girl is, I hope that she does love that hair. I hope that she feels as beautiful as I did when it was mine.

The ponytail was placed in a plastic bag to be shipped and my friend began to style my hair. I never would have thought I could feel pretty again, but I felt even more beautiful than before. I went home that night, took a bunch of pictures, and posted them on Facebook. Everyone was so supportive and cheered me on. I had "a new hope" and I felt like I could take on the world.

A few weeks later, work let out for Christmas break. I kept my social life alive and hung out with family and friends as much as I could. Everything was feeling pretty normal, despite my symptoms. On Christmas morning, my brother and I stocked up on Doctor Who gifts and I got an iPad to start writing my book. You are experiencing book-ception because I'm using my iPad now to write these words. It wasn't until a few days later that I realized that the rest of my hair was going to have to go. I was combing it in the bathroom when a large chunk fell off my head and into the sink. I had been losing a little bit more than normal the entire week, but nothing like I had that day. My hair steadily fell out for the next three days. It fell behind me like a trail of breadcrumbs everywhere I went. It felt like I was in some sort of horror film while I was showering because my hair was coming off in my hands. I quickly clogged most of the sinks in the house and my family had to stock up on drain cleaner. I kept my cool and I started getting annoyed with my hair more than anything. I finally decided to call my stylist and set up an appointment for the following Saturday for the pixie cut. One of my close friends really wanted to support me during the challenge of losing my hair. When it came time to take on the pixie cut, she insisted that she wanted to be there beside me, getting her own locks cut. Being an extreme Encourager, my friend sat in the battle with me as we both faced our shears.

My stylist began combing my hair, pulling out any loose strands. My hair came out in massive chunks and completely littered the floor. I felt like Gollum from *Lord of the Rings*. My hair hung around my face in stringy locks. I was "Stringylocks" and cancer was The Three Bears. I felt so ugly, but I knew that this look was only temporary. My stylist continued to cut my hair into the pixie cut and tried her best to make it look presentable. My scalp was littered with bald spots, most of which were on the very top of my head. I did not cry, as I had when I first cut my hair. I was done crying about the tangled strands I left on the floor. I just wanted to stop dealing with it.

My friend was next in line to get her hair cut and if she was nervous, she did not show it. She showed a picture of Keira Knightley to my stylist as she put her ponytail into rubber bands like she had for mine. She was able to give another 13-inch ponytail to Locks of Love and she looked stunning in her new hairdo. My Mom took a million pictures of us after we left the little salon. We were laughing and smiling at the camera, as I left hairs in my wake and tried to hide my embarrassment. After our makeshift photoshoot, we went to the mall to get my friend some beauty supplies for her new hairstyle. I did not buy any, though. I knew my hair would be mostly gone by morning. The next day, I woke lying in heaps of little hairs on my pillow. The bald spot on the top of my head had become obnoxiously large, so I put on a hat and headed to church. I explained to a few friends what happened at the salon and showed them my dreaded bald spot. I told them that I just wanted to shave my head as soon as possible.

My friends came through that day with an amazing act of kindness. One of them decided to shave his head alongside me and I quickly agreed. Anxious, I asked him if we could shave our heads that same day and we headed to my house for a shaving party. To this day I feel badly for springing the shaving party on my Mom last minute; I was so wrapped up in how I felt that I did not think to ask her how she might be feeling. It was a horrible experience for her to have to shave her daughter's head, and I did not realize it until I had reflected on it months later. Thankfully, my Mom is a warrior. She shaved my head without hesitation and did not say a word.

My Mom then moved on to my friend. I rubbed my fuzzy head and watched as my friend's blonde hair hit the floor. He kept his eyes focused and did not say a word. His wife and I, on the other hand, could not stop smiling. Between the two of us, we took at least a hundred pictures. We then took turns shaving sections of his head and it was obvious we were having a lot more fun than he was. I was no longer plagued with little hairs falling into my eyes constantly and getting stuck in my eyebrows. It felt liberating. At the end of the evening, hair was everywhere, friends were together, and I felt ready to tackle the next chapter of the cancer story.

Two days after I shaved my head, I went into the clinic for my second round of chemo. I had been dreading returning to the chamber of chemo and I struggled with chemo nightmares leading up to it. I sat in my pod next to some lovely older ladies with breast cancer. They told me that I was pretty as a bald woman and that I had a good-shaped head. It was not the last time someone commented on the shape of my skull.

My brother and friend brought lunch and came up to hang out for a while. We were loud and laughing obnoxiously, although we were trying our best to keep it cool. That's when we discovered the private rooms. I had always wondered what was beyond those doors, but I had not yet discovered their secrets until that day. I was excited when a nurse came over and offered a private room for my next round.

The following day was New Year's Eve. After a nauseous night with tingly arms, I spent the entire day getting ready to go out. It took me hours to put on my wig and do my makeup. Your body moves at the speed of molasses after chemo and your arms become as heavy as elephant tusks. I took frequent breaks between mascara, blush and gluing my fake scalp onto my head. Finally, I felt presentable and hopped in my car to meet up with friends downtown. When you have cancer, you wind up driving yourself places because you want to be able to leave when you get sick. The last thing I wanted was to make my friends drive me home on New Year's Eve.

We headed to a sushi restaurant. When you're on chemo, you're not allowed to eat sushi or drink alcohol, so I stared longingly at the California rolls. A friend of mine paid for my meal and kept it a secret until long after the bills had come and gone. It was super-nice and I was not expecting it. After stuffing my face with noodles, we headed to an apartment for a party. Everything was going great until I walked in and looked up at the ceiling. If cancer wasn't going to kill me, the hundreds of balloons hanging in a net over my head would. If I haven't mentioned it before, I am extremely allergic to latex. My plan was to stand in the hallway outside the apartment at midnight while everyone danced under the balloons and kissed each other. Little did I know that when a friend realized what was going on, he decided to take matters into his own hands. Once the balloons dropped and everyone had traditionally slobbered on one another, I heard him start yelling. He threw open the windows of the tall apartment building and started shouting, "Save JoAnna!" while throwing balloons out on to the street below. Everyone joined in, yelling his catch phrase and throwing balloons out the windows. I was laughing and smiling because of the ridiculousness of it all and the fact that most of the people yelling my name did not know me. I'm sure it must have been magical for the people below, walking along the street being rained on by hundreds of balloons. It wound up being the highlight of the night and I was invited back for the following year. I went home shortly after midnight, exhausted and needing to at least get out of bed the next day. It had been a great night despite the fight with cancer. At the end of the evening, the tingly feeling in my arms was gone and I felt nauseous and ready for bed. My New Year's resolution was: kick cancer's ass.

"Cancer messes you up a little and that's okay."

CHAPTER 5.5

How to Lose Your Hair with Style and Grace

When undergoing cancer treatment, there is a possibility that you may lose your hair. What some people do not understand is that the chemo you take makes your hair fall out, not the actual cancer. When I explained this to my students, I told them that when I was bald it meant that I was getting better. Hair is nothing more than a bunch of dead skin cells, clumped together to form strands of color. Chemotherapy gets rid of infected and dead cells in your body. This makes your hair a natural target for chemical warfare. You are going to have an opportunity to grow back amazing and beautiful hair after your battle is over. It may even come back a different color, texture, or covered in curls, if you are lucky. Before chemo, my hair was light brown, stick straight, and very thin. After chemo, my hair came back dark brown, full of waves, and much thicker. It is a thousand times better now than it was before.

I took my new growth as an opportunity to take better care of my hair. I stopped coloring, curling, and using products full of wax and chemicals. I now use only natural products and the days of dying my ends are over, at least until I go gray. You have a lot to look forward to when it comes to growing your hair back, but for now, let's talk about what to expect when you lose your hair and how to rock the bald look. If you're a guy, do not think that this does not apply to you. Hair loss sucks for everyone. Can you imagine what it would be like if Thor lost his locks? It would be devastating! So, yes, guys also care about their hair. Some guys even spend 20 minutes making it look like they just woke up, but us ladies know better. With that being said, there are options available for both genders in the hair department. If you go to a hair salon that sells wigs made with human hair, they have options available that are so realistic, it's scary. I found myself wondering who else in this world is walking around fooling everyone.

If you have not started chemo yet or if you are completely bald already, losing your hair is not something to be ashamed of. Your body is in the midst of the fight for its life and you will have outward signs of an inward battle. Aside from being bald, some treatments may require you to get a tattoo to mark areas for radiation treatment. More than likely you'll acquire some pretty epic scars. Cancer makes a person tough. Cancer patients are commonly people with bald heads, bruises, scars and possibly tattoos. You are one motorcycle away from being in the *Sons of Anarchy*. If you still have hair, then you need to plan out how you would like to lose it gracefully. I decided to go through stages of haircuts before I finally shaved it off. For people with shorter hair already, I would recommend cutting it down slowly. If your hair is long and luscious, it will be more of a process.

Stage 1 – The Quarter Cut
If you have long hair, I strongly suggest getting the chin-length bob first. If you would like, you can harvest the remains for Locks of Love and donate it to someone in need. There are also companies that will make a wig for you from your own hair. Do some research to find what is best for you.

Stage 2 – The Pixie
The biggest mistake I made was waiting too long to go for the pixie cut. I wish I would have gotten it a week earlier when I first started noticing my hair falling out. Unfortunately, I was too nervous and I waited. As a result, I only got to enjoy the cut for 12 hours and it was not as full as it could have been.

Stage 3 – The Shave
Shave your head when the little hairs falling out of your head are too much to bare. Toward the end of the hair-losing process, I was very excited to buzz my head.

Stage 4 – Let It Go
Let it go. Let it go. Can't have hair anymore. Let it go. Let it go. Shave away and cover the floor. I don't care what they're going to say! Let the bald rage on! The breeze never bothered me anyway. At this point, the little buzzed hairs on your head will all fall out.

The following timeline from my cancer diary will give you a better idea of what to expect. I started losing my hair two weeks after my first chemo and it happened over the course of 7 days. There are stages you will go through before it completely falls out:

1. A Tender Head
First, your head will begin to hurt, feeling tight and soft all over. It is normal,

but it does indicate that you only have a few days left until it starts to fall out.

2. An Itchy Scalp
Next, your head will start to itch. You will want to scratch it, but do not, because it will be tender and painful. This feeling will go away once it all falls out.

3. Lose a Few
Your hair will slowly start to fall out 2 to 3 days after it becomes tender and itchy. You will begin to leave trails of hair behind you like Hansel and Gretel leaving breadcrumbs.

4. Lose a Lot
On day 4 or 5, your hair will start to fall out in larger clumps. You will want to put a cover on your shower drain to catch it or you will get a clogged pipe or two.

5. Gollum
Days 5 through 7, your head will start to look like Gollum, the sickly creature from *Lord of the Rings*. At this point, you might want to think about shaving it because if you do not, people are going to start asking you if you found the Precious.

I started noticing a tender scalp on a Monday and I finally shaved it off on the following Sunday. Everyone is different and each person will lose their hair in different ways. This was my personal experience, but a few of my friends experienced the same pattern. Losing your hair is always going to be a big part of your story. It was the worst part for me emotionally. After I was done with chemo, areas of my hair began growing back at different rates. The back of my head grew hair much faster than the sides and, for a while, I sported a righteous mullet. My Mom offered to shave up the scraggly hairs on the base of my neck. When she turned on the razor, I started to cry and backed out of the room like she was coming at me with a machete. Cancer messes you up a little and that's okay. We are all a little messed up in our own way. I continued growing my hair and waited for a few months before I finally gained the courage I needed to get a proper haircut. I spent many months looking like a scruffy nerf herder.

"At this point in the process, I stopped caring about what I looked like."

CHAPTER 6

Valentine's Day Rollercoaster Ride

Life continued on as normal. I went back to work, attended meetings, filled out paperwork and continued to teach my students. When I got back to school, my co-workers told me we had a meeting after the kids left school and I did not want to go. Finally, one of them told me there would be food and so I decided a meeting no longer sounded terrible. I headed down to the library and immediately stepped into the food line to pile little sausages onto my plate. When I turned around to find a seat, I saw a Gryffindor hat and scarf sitting on a nearby table. I looked at the ladies sitting there, each of them beaming at me. My "chemo brain" was extra slow that day. I stammered a ridiculous comment about being sorted into Gryffindor and made my way to a table.

It was not until I sat down that I finally realized that there were hats and scarves on every table and that everyone was looking at me. I was sitting at a surprise hat party and I was the guest of honor. I stood up, holding my little sausages on my styrofoam plate and cried while everyone clapped and cheered. When I say I worked with the best staff in the world, I mean it. I received a dozen hats, including one that looked like Yoda and each had a scarf to match. I could not believe it. I realized then that I must really be in a daze. You stop paying attention to most things when you are on chemo, with the exception of how you feel and where the bathrooms are.

The kindness and awesome outreaches did not stop there. During the beginning of the new year, my friends were so generous, surprising me with gifts and food. I received cookies, a nerdy gift basket, blankets, and other fun things. I was so grateful to have everyone's support. On top of gaining weight from the roids, I gained cookie weight, too. It was around this time that I started feeling like an actual cancer patient. I was blown up like a balloon, bald as Mr. Clean and I had about ten eyelashes left on each eye. At this point in the process, I stopped caring about what I looked like. I made sure I did not leave the house in my pajamas, but that was the extent of my effort to look presentable. People would stare at me, but I tried not to notice. It still hurt to look in the mirror but the drive to fix myself up every day had vanished.

This sudden change in my self-image was accompanied by another blow to the ego, Valentine's Day. I would be spending Valentine's Day hooking up with my favorite lover ... R-CHOP. I had not dated since before I was diagnosed and I was not dating during cancer. It was convenient to not have to worry about how I looked, but I still wished I had someone worth the struggle of applying makeup. On Valentine's Day, flying solo is usually hard for most people and for me this was no exception. A few days shy of Valentine's Day I walked into the cancer clinic without my usual entourage. For reasons unknown, my friends were all busy and no one could come hang out in my private room. It was a bummer, but the nurses insisted that I have my own room, anyway. Sighing, I opened the door and prepared myself for six hours in the lonely-hearts club. To my surprise, when I opened the door I heard, "I came to warm your seat up, baby!" My Aunt Ginger smiled, curled up in a blanket as she sat in my chemo recliner.

I was completely dumbfounded. I hadn't seen my Aunt in years and I was not expecting her to be in Kansas City all the way from California. Nurses were gathered outside the room and my Mom and uncle were capturing the moment on film. There was not a dry eye all around us as we hugged each other and I sobbed loudly on her shoulder. My Aunt and I spent the next few hours catching up. We laughed, ate Steak n Shake and for a while I did not feel like I had cancer anymore. Everything was going great until I noticed my vision was fading. Squiggly lines formed all across my field of vision. I did not mention it for several minutes because it was such a perfect day. I did not want to ruin it because of a stupid symptom that I thought would quickly pass. Finally, I decided I should say something and the nurses quickly pulled up the computer to start googling symptoms. Immediately, my doctor ordered one of my meds to be cut off and ushered my Aunt and I out the door. We were then sent to an eye specialist in the heart of downtown. Once I got there, the ophthalmologist dilated my eyes and took pictures. It was a strange experience having my eyes dilated while viewing the world through squiggle-vision.

My Aunt was worried sick, running back and forth, calling doctors, and going to get snacks for me to consume. After the doctor took pictures of the back of my eyes, I sat patiently in a tiny room, dangling my feet and humming to myself. After a grueling wait, the doctor gave me the all-clear and told me to finish my chemo the next day. At the time, I had not been told that there was a chance that I could have suffered a stroke. I was the first documented person to have that particular symptom. That night, I was exhausted, but I wanted to spend more time with my Aunt and family. She got me a pizza and I almost ate the entire thing by myself before heading home. That night I laid in bed with a smile on my face and a tingle in my arms.

The next day I went to the Cancer Center to finish my chemo and get on with my weekend. I put on make-up that morning and, looking back, I'm very happy I did. It was not long after I got hooked up that a one-man news crew showed up from a local television station with a camera, microphone and a few questions. The director of the center had called the local news station and told them my story. The director told me that she was inspired by my drive, charisma and my plans for this book. She wanted to share my story with others and I was honored to do so. The reporter interviewed me for an hour about my life and ambitions. I could not believe that any of it was happening. I felt honored and most of all, I felt famous. That night, my family gathered and watched my two-minute news segment. My Facebook and phone started flooding with messages from friends and family, telling me that they had seen me on the news. I had a mixture of emotions: I was happy, nervous, and a little sick to my stomach with all the attention. The phone calls and messages continued throughout the weekend and my time with my Aunt and family came to an end. The celebrity status finally died down after a couple of weeks.

"Cancer may be the biggest part of your life currently, but it is not who you are."

CHAPTER 6.5

Dating

After having experienced a romantic Valentine's Day with Mr. Chemo Therapy, I want to address the frustrating subject of dating while fighting cancer. I can understand how it would be difficult to see the person you have feelings for everyday while you are bald and your weight is out of control. I was fortunate enough to not have to face the person that I had feelings for very often, but I can imagine how difficult it must be. If you are confident in continuing to date, go for it! Cancer may be part of your life but it is not your whole life. Cancer does not mean you should stop dating. Even though you can choose to continue dating, your life has changed, which means your dating life has changed, too. Whether you are going on dates with a long-term significant other, your spouse, or someone new, there are a few rules to live by now that you are dating with cancer.

The Ten Commandments of Dating
If you are going on a date, it is important for you to treat yourself to a new outfit. More than likely your clothes will no longer fit. This is a great opportunity for retail therapy and a new outfit will help boost your confidence.

Wear your wig. It might be a hassle, but you will not regret it. Wearing your wig will help both you and your date to relax and focus on each other. Glue on your wig and give it a tug to make sure it's secure. It is better to have your wig glued down and avoid a wardrobe malfunction.

P.S. Make sure to warn your significant other that you are wearing a wig. It is better that they know not to pull on your hair than to have them unintentionally pull it off.

Give yourself plenty of time to get ready for your date. If you have post-chemo tingly arms, it will be difficult to get ready quickly. If you have plenty of time, you can take breaks.

If you are not feeling well, stay close to home or stay in completely. You do not want to be out and get stuck in a public restroom. It is possible to modify your date night by eating nearby or ordering take out. Cancer should not be allowed to ruin your fun and there's nothing wrong with staying home with a pizza and a movie on TV.

No raw sushi. You doctor will advise you to not eat sushi when you are on chemo. Raw fish can be dangerous for your immune system and it is better to avoid it altogether unless the fish is fully cooked. Think about your body when choosing a restaurant. Make sure you will not be stuck eating any type of food that could make you sick.

No alcohol. Your doctor will also advise you to not drink alcohol while receiving treatment. Alcohol can interfere with the way chemotherapy works and possibly cause it to be ineffective. A small amount on special occasions may be fine, but it is better to speak with your doctor first.

Be careful when choosing a movie. Chemotherapy will sometimes make you more emotional. If you would rather not ball like a baby in front of your date, be careful about which movie you choose. This meant no Disney movies for me while I was on chemo.

Cancer may be the biggest part of your life currently, but it is not who you are. Try not to talk about your cancer. You are an incredible, interesting human being. You are far more than your diagnosis. On date night, talk about what you would have talked about before you got sick (movies, sports, celebrities, etc.).

Your port is going to stick out and feel strange under your skin. A lot of people will want to touch it, especially your family and friends. Before letting your date feel around on your body, warn him or her that you have a small Arch Reactor on the inside of your chest. It may kill the mood if they discover a piece of hardware under your skin without warning. Other people could feel my port even just by giving me a hug, so it's better to let them know ahead of time.

You and your significant other can take cancer as an opportunity to be more proactive about preventative measures. It may not seem romantic, but you can help each other self-check for many types of cancer. Have your significant other help check you for lumps and bumps. It will be both steamy and beneficial to your health.

Most everyone dreams about finding love and I'm no exception. During chemo, however, I did not want to develop a love life. Even though I might not have been actively seeking out a romance, it did not stop young men from calling on me. Freely date whoever you choose, but keep an eye out for people whose feelings developed after you were diagnosed. I encountered a plethora of strange individuals who were more interested in the "girl with cancer" than JoAnna. These young men used cancer to try to date me and they were individuals who would not have normally pursued me. Some of them used cancer as an excuse to strike up a conversation or as a basis for their "undying love." The point is, be careful when someone starts showing interest. Make sure they are legit. If they are not legit, you must quit.

Some people simply cannot handle themselves in any situation. One night after work, some friends and I decided to go to Steak n' Shake. We sat down at our table and a young man, clearly hungover, came to take our order. He began the conversation by saying, "I'm Bryan and I was at duh strip club downtown all night so I'm hungover. What cha drinkin' on?" We all whispered, "water," and watched him stagger away. As he turned the corner, we started laughing and began conspiring ways to pull one over on him. After he put down our waters and scribbled down our orders, he was gone for quite some time. Finally, he returned with our food and, as soon as he put my food in front of me, I said, "Thank you," while pulling off my hat and staring at him in all my bald glory. Immediately, he slurred out the words, "Oh s**t" and stumbled awkwardly backward into the kitchen. For the rest of the evening we sat there eating happily, while Bryan awkwardly avoided me, too frightened to make eye contact. We laughed the rest of the night, knowing that he probably thought he smoked a bad batch of weed.

People like Bryan help you appreciate people who are not like Bryan. Cancer is similar in that way because it helps you appreciate things that are not cancer. You appreciate your life before cancer and you will appreciate your life after cancer. Relationships come and go. Some only for a few months and some forever. When you are sick, you start to appreciate your time and you only want to share it with the ones who matter most. The moral of the story is, whether or not you date is completely up to you. Having cancer helps you appreciate relationships and in the end, your relationships are what matters most.

"My beliefs gave me the hope of a life after death."

CHAPTER 7

What to Do If You Are Terminal

If the odds are not in your favor, you may find yourself thinking about some of life's biggest questions. When you are told that you may have only weeks or months to live, you stop caring about some of the ridiculous things in life. Life has thrown you a curveball called cancer, but that does not mean that a statistic or a projected expiration date is set in stone. Miracles happen, hope carries us through the darkest of times, and we should never give up. As Han Solo said, "Never tell me the odds!" Cancer helps you appreciate life. This is an opportunity to resolve certain issues with the time that you have. Whether that time is 20 days or 20 years (and really, whether you have cancer or not), you should spend every moment living a life that is knee-deep in purpose and love. Here are some ideas to consider when you are contemplating life's complexities:

1. Right now is a great time to start mending relationships and righting your wrongs. Relationships are too important to leave broken in this life. Even if you are right and the other person is wrong, be the bigger person and reach out to them.

2. Have a living will and testament. It may be morbid, but many people have one and it will save your family from a lot of stress, arguments and legal fees.

3. Start seeking out the answers to your questions about life. Death is the next great adventure, but what exactly happens? Many people find comfort and hope as they look for answers. A lot of people turn to religion or seek knowledge from people they know and trust.

As you search for the answers to life's big questions, you will come across many different religions and theories. When I was faced with these questions, I knew I had nothing to fear. My beliefs gave me the hope of a life after death. When my Dad passed away, I knew I would one day see him again. Death never scared me because I understood what would happen to me after I died.

My Christian faith has always been the biggest part of my life, both before and after cancer. I believe that God loves me and has a place waiting for me after I die. After accepting my beliefs as truth, I now have security in life after death and reuniting with my family in heaven. It was this hope that fueled my desire to live life fully during my cancer treatment and focus less on what would happen to me after I died and more on what I could do with the time I have.

During my cancer treatments, my purpose for living was made clear, I was created to show God's love to others. I find that, by focusing my energy externally in helping other people, I am able to live a fulfilled and happy life. If you have not already, start searching for the answers to your questions. You are important, and you were not put on this earth by accident. Everyone has been created individually and for a certain purpose. The hairs on your head are numbered and you are loved beyond anything that you can comprehend. You can use the Bible passages I list below if you would like to know more about my beliefs and who God is. Find a Bible in your home, at a bookstore, or download the YouVersion Bible app on your smartphone and you will be able to begin on your journey.

– Start by reading through the book of John. Most of your answers will come directly from this book of the Bible. John talks about basic beliefs, including the story of who God is, how He loves us, and what He has done for us.

– The Romans Road is an outline explaining what it means to accept God's offer of salvation. He has a lot in store of you and these verses will explain to you how you can start living life with God by your side: Romans 3:23, Romans 6:23, Romans 5:8, Romans 10:9, Romans 10:13, Romans 5:1

– There are many verses about life after death and the promises of what heaven will be like: John 14:3, Revelation 21:4, 2 Corinthians 5:8, Philippians 3:20-21

I hope that you will find answers to your questions and peace in what life is like after death. The next chapters of this book are about life after cancer. They talk about what to expect as you step back into normalcy and all the struggles that come with it. There are many people who will eventually find themselves in a place of remission, but there are also those who may not make it that far. Either way, you need to fight the good fight. Be prepared for anything that may happen, but never give up.

"Of all the battles I knew I would face during cancer, I never expected this."

CHAPTER 8

After Cancer and Beyond

After a few more rounds of chemo, I was finally ready for my last treatment. I felt like I had been crawling to the finish line, but I was finally there. I knew I would still have to do a CT scan to make sure the tumors were gone, but I would not be returning to the tiny private room that I had made my home away from home. After they unplugged me from my machine for the last time, I was honored with a goodbye ceremony from the staff. I was given a chemo certificate of completion and I rang the old-fashioned bell by the door that signaled the end. The three weeks in between my last chemo and my next CT scan were the most mentally draining. All I thought and dreamed about was a clean scan. I was eager at the thought of starting my life anew and I just needed my doctor's approval.

My scans came back clear and I was set free! My family laughed and cried tears of happiness. We left the clinic ready to take on the world, but I was naive to think the trials were over. The healing process had just begun. Every month I went back into the clinic to have my port flushed. The nurse would put a syringe of saline into my port to keep it clear from build-up. I was also scheduled to have blood work done every three months and a full body scan every six months for a few years.

After letting my friends know I was in remission on Facebook, my phone rang with encouraging texts and congratulatory phone calls. A month later, school let out for summer break and I was ready to have fun. Thankfully, my hair had grown in a little (about a half an inch) so I was feeling more confident and I stopped wearing hats. I did not think I had the cheek bones to go with the pixie style, but everyone else said they really liked it. Aside from my hair, my biggest insecurity was still my weight. I had not dropped an ounce from the thirty pounds I had gained during chemo treatments. Summer was here and I was in no hurry to parade around in a yellow polka-dot bikini. I was in desperate need of a wardrobe change.

Cancer had stolen my life and I was ready to get it back. I quickly realized this is never a good tactic if your body is healing from major chemical warfare. I was so excited to have my old body back, that I neglected the words "one-year recovery time," "steroid weight," and "up to a year until you see a difference." I began a popular prepackaged food diet the day after my last chemo. It was the worst mistake I made during the whole process. I starved myself for two weeks trying to only eat the small pre-made foods, pretending I felt better. At the end of two weeks, I had gained four pounds even after eating very small portions and I felt worse than before.

I had tried and failed to get my old body back. I was too eager and I overlooked the fact that I was still recovering from my last treatment. I decided to rekindle my efforts one month later. Instead of starving myself, I cut down on sodium and I started eating organic foods. I started walking every day, eating lots of vegetables, and I got plenty of sunshine.

Even though I loved shopping, it took a while for me to feel comfortable enough to walk into a store. I felt awkward in my body and I knew I would have to buy sizes I was not accustomed to. After a few weeks, my Mom and I decided to take a day trip down to the Lake of the Ozarks to visit some of our beloved outlets. I had finally built up the confidence I needed to take on the department stores. I was so excited to walk into the fluorescent lighting, run my hands through the racks of clothing and try on a million pairs of shoes. Instead, I spent the day realizing that there are two sides to the human race and one side of it is not so pleasant.

It is a well-known stigma that some women in the homosexual/transgender community wear their hair a bit shorter. I knew that I would go through a "Lesbian hair stage," but I did not know that people would treat me differently because of it. For the first time in my life, I was punished and shunned in a way that made me want to shut myself in my room and never come out. The worst part was, I was treated this way by girls who looked the way I used to look before I started cancer treatments. It was the pretty, thin girls with long, beautiful hair that hurt me the most.

My mom and I began our shopping spree at the Nautica outlet. I was greeted by a young girl who looked to be in her early twenties. She was pretty much like any other college girl and she had gorgeous, long brown hair. She was folding clothes by the front door when we walked in. She did not look up as she started to say, "Hello, welcome to Nautica, do you need any…" and then cut herself off when she finally saw me. Immediately after looking at me, her face contorted in horror and she backed away from me as if I had the plague. I looked down at the ground and fought back the tears welling up in my eyes. My Mom stood beside me mortified and I tugged on her arm and whispered a plea to leave the store. The girl retreated to the back of the room and I heard her giggling with another girl and looking in my direction. My Mom was furious and I could see heat rising in her cheeks. My Mom grabbed my hand and pulled me towards the other side of the store. She told me not to let girls like that get to me, but it was too late. After that day, I learned to shy away from pretty girls as a defense mechanism. Of all the battles I knew I would face during cancer, I never expected this.

While my hair was short, I was mistreated almost everywhere I went. I had never felt judged by anyone before, but I was starting to realize how often it happens and how horrible it feels. The worst encounter happened at my primary doctor's office a few days after my shopping trip. After recording my height and weight, the nurse assistant rolled her eyes at me and strapped the blue pressure cuff on my arm. The nurse was in her early twenties and she had long blonde hair. Finally, she asked for my past medical history. Her attitude completely changed as I explained my history of lymphoma. After that moment, you would have thought she was in an audition to be my best friend. I was polite and smiled, but inside my blood was boiling. The trend continued and I began to feel isolated and lonely. I wanted to hug every short-haired girl I saw because I did not care if she was a lesbian, cancer survivor or just trendy; no one should be treated the way I was. It was not until my hair had grown out over an inch that the cruelty I received from young women finally began to die down.

I continued to let my hair grow a few more inches during the next couple of months before I was able to build up the courage I needed to get my first haircut. The tips of my hair were white and for a while, we thought it might be growing back blonde. We found out later that the white tips were only dead strands that grew in colorless because of a chemical reaction from chemo. At the time, I was rocking a mullet that would make Joe Dirt jealous. The back of my hair grew much faster than the front, touching my shoulders. Every day I pulled the mullet into a ponytail until my Mom convinced me it was time to get my hair cut and styled. My first haircut was difficult. I hyperventilated at the buzz of trimmers in the background and cried rivers of tears as the scissors cut through my baby strands. I ended the appointment with an inverted bob and

I let my hair grow out again before the next cut.

Getting my hair cut is still a challenge. I no longer cry, but the sound of the trimmer makes me cringe and clench my fists. I am able to cope with it and I know that the sounds will not bug me forever. My weight issue was not resolved as quickly as I would have liked. Eighteen months later, my weight was down but I was by no means back to my pre-cancer body. The doctor told me that the weight put on by steroids is different for everyone. Some people have steroid weight melt off and others have to let it linger.

I had my port removed before I left Kansas City to start a new chapter of life in San Diego. Like a cut from a Morgul blade (and ironically in the same place as Frodo's wound), the scar from my port continues to hurt at random moments in time. The doctor said that it is normal for the scar tissue to hurt sporadically for years after removing it. When it starts to hurt, I sometimes grab my chest and tell my family that, "My scar hurts. Voldemort's near." We all laugh and it helps dull the pain.

After cancer treatments, you must remember your body has just gone through hell and back in the form of physical and chemical warfare. The biggest lesson that I learned from my post-cancer experience was that I should give myself a break. I was way too hard on myself after chemo. I expected to quickly revert back to the old me but I can never go back to who I was before cancer. Circumstances change a person and sometimes it is for the better. I am more accepting and thankful now for the way my body looks and feels.

"You are not alone in this."

CHAPTER 9

The Aftermath

Life after cancer is a series of ups and downs. The road evens out eventually, but you will find yourself on a very different ride than before you were diagnosed. Your emotional and mental health may be affected in ways you would not have expected. Below, I have highlighted specific things you should keep in mind after you are finished with chemo. I have also listed items that I struggled with mentally and emotionally in the months following my last treatment. Everyone is different, so these difficulties may not relate easily to your own struggles, but I hope by sharing them with you, that you will better understand how you may be thinking and feeling.

Always . . .

Make sure you have an oncologist. This means if you ever move out of the city, state, or even country, your first medical priority should be establishing with an awesome oncologist.

Keep up with your scans and blood work. Check in with your doctor and set up your appointments at least a month in advance.

Talk to your doctor about how you are feeling. Every time you have the sniffles it does not mean that you have cancer, but it is better to be safe than sorry.

Take care of your new baby hair. Your hair is going to be soft and new like an infant. If you are a person who constantly color-treated and flat-ironed your hair like I did, it is your chance to do something new. Take care of your hair! Try to steer clear of thick shampoos. Clear or semi-transparent shampoos have less wax in them and are healthier for your locks. Now would also be a good time to wash your hair less often. For example, I wash mine every other day, but everyone's hair is different and you may not need to wash yours as often.

Take care of your mental and emotional health. You are not alone in this. Listed below are my personal thoughts and feelings. Some of these have been temporary, some are still with me today. Everyone is different, we all heal at different rates and the brain is no exception:

1. Counting hairs – After my hair started growing back, I began counting the number of hairs that I would lose during my showers. I did not like losing any baby hair from my head. Even though I knew that it is normal to lose hair, I had horrible flashbacks of when I started losing all of my hair from the first round of chemo.

2. Needle annoyance – After getting poked and prodded with needles so often, you start to get annoyed by them. You may try to avoid them, not because they hurt, but because you are tired of getting stuck. You may not be the first to get in line for your flu shot this year.

3. Crying at awkward moments – After chemo, I would get teary-eyed when people mentioned steroids. I would get emotional when I watched sad television commercials. I was a walking rain cloud for a few months. Crying is healthy and normal. Never force yourself to stop. Let the tears flow and know that it is okay to have a good cry.

4. Medicine – When I was finally free from all my prescriptions, the last thing I wanted to do was take more medication. I used to take medicine often for headaches, sinus pressure, etc., but after chemo, I was much more cautious, for my liver's sake, about taking anything. I wanted everything out of my body and I did not start taking over the counter medications until one year after chemo.

5. Self-image issues – I will often see a big, bald babe staring back at me in the mirror. We do not perceive ourselves the way that others do, but that is completely normal. It takes time to learn to love yourself and your body. Focus on maintaining a healthy lifestyle and self-image issues will be easier to handle.

6. Thinking everything is cancer – After you have had cancer, you think every feeling may be a symptom. Every time I had the flu or had a hot flash, I wanted to get a scan. It is good to be proactive, but you do not need to be over-reactive. Your sore legs may be from the hike you took yesterday and your headache is probably just nasal congestion. If you are really concerned, talk to your doctor about what you are feeling, but keep in mind that not everything is cancer.

7. Cancer nightmares – While I was fighting cancer, I had chemo-symptom nightmares. I would dream about being hooked up at the cancer clinic or watching my hair fall out again. I still have these dreams, but they are much less frequent.

8. Creature Comforts – Before cancer, I was footloose and fancy-free. I would sleep on my friend's sofa, eat dinner late at night and travel alone to visit friends and family. For three months after chemo, I would have anxiety about sleeping in my own bed and eating my meals on a set schedule. I felt unsafe to be out in public alone and I did not strike up conversations with strangers the way that I used to. Thankfully, that phase is over.

9. Family Matters – I wasn't the only one affected by these emotional and mental issues. To this day, my brother still fears going to the doctor because he is afraid he will end up with cancer too. And every time there is something wrong with me, my family and my doctors rush me off to the hospital for tests. Family and friends may develop their own cancer fears for themselves and you, so it is best to be sensitive and support as they work these feelings and thoughts out.

10. No More Risky Business – After surviving a life threatening illness, you stop taking risks. I started being afraid of heights and I lost my curious, daredevil streak that would flow through my veins. I don't take risks like I used to and I now think through every possible outcome before taking action. This is normal for survivors but it took me awhile to accept it. I am now the Neville Longbottom of Gryffindors (but it worked out very well for him in the end).

You may have a few extra bags that you will carry with you from this point on. Whether it is counting hairs or crying during commercials, you are not alone and more importantly, you are not crazy. It is normal to need help during and after fighting cancer. There are many people that you can seek out for help if you are feeling overwhelmed by your new thoughts and emotions. You can meet with a family member, friend, or religious leader to help you talk through your experiences. Check online for local cancer centers, psychologists, and support groups.

Everyone handles traumatic events differently. Like any war, there are things that you will carry with you long after you have left the battlefield. You will wear these scars forever and harbor memories that you would rather forget. There is light at the end of this tunnel. You will be happy again, you will be healthy again, and you will reclaim your life. It takes time, but never give up hope. The words I took with me throughout my cancer experience and beyond were spoken by Samwise Gamgee of the Shire:

"Even darkness must pass. A new day will come.
And when the sun shines, it will shine out the clearer."

"Never give up, never surrender,"
—Commander Peter Quincy Taggart.

CHAPTER 10

The End

This is the end of our time together. Thank you for allowing me to share with you what I have learned during my own journey. I know it has been a wild ride and that you have had to take in a lot of information but I appreciate your willingness to learn with me through your own personal struggle. I'm not saying it is going to be easy getting over cancer. Surviving a deadly illness is not easy, but you are not alone. There are plenty of people in this world who understand your struggles because they have been there themselves. Cancer may be a small chapter in your life or an on-going saga. Either way, I encourage you to put on your armor and wield your sword. This battle for your life is worth fighting. It is my hope that this book has provided you with clarity and has encouraged you to keep moving forward. I cannot claim to know everything, but I do know some things. I want you to have as much wisdom as I can offer so I wrote these pages with you in mind and I will keep you in my thoughts and prayers. Keep your eyes focused, brave the storm, and kick cancer's ass.

–JoAnna Barker

http://fox4kc.com/2014/02/14/blue-springs-teacher-chronicling-her-battle-against-cancer/

Made in the USA
Monee, IL
28 March 2021